THE
RELIANCE
BUILDING

A BUILDING BOOK FROM
THE CHICAGO
ARCHITECTURE FOUNDATION

JAY PRIDMORE

PHOTOGRAPHS BY
HEDRICH BLESSING

Pomegranate

SAN FRANCISCO

Published by Pomegranate Communications, Inc.
Box 6099, Rohnert Park, California 94927
800 227 1428; www.pomegranate.com

Pomegranate Europe Ltd.
Unit 1, Heathcote Business Centre, Hurlbutt Road
Warwick, Warwickshire CV34 6TD U. K.

Library of Congress Cataloging-in-Publication Data
Pridmore, Jay.
    The Reliance Building : a building book from the Chicago Architecture Foundation/
Jay Pridmore ; photographs by Hedrich Blessing.
        p. cm.
    ISBN 0-7649-2307-2 (alk. paper)
        1. Reliance Building (Chicago, Ill.) 2. Burnham and Root. 3. Chicago (Ill.) — Buildings, structures, etc. I. Blessing, Hedrich. II. Chicago Architecture Foundation. III. Title.

NA6233.C4 R447 2003
720'.9773'11 — dc21

                                                                            2002030784

Pomegranate Catalog No. A661

Cover and book design by Shannon Lemme

Printed in Korea

10 09 08 07 06 05 04 03   10 9 8 7 6 5 4 3 2 1

Mission

The Chicago Architecture Foundation (CAF) is dedicated to advancing public interest and education in architecture and related design. CAF pursues this mission through a comprehensive program of tours, lectures, exhibitions, special programs, and youth programs, all designed to enhance the public's awareness and appreciation of Chicago's important architectural legacy.

Founded in 1966, the Chicago Architecture Foundation has evolved to become a nationally recognized resource advancing public interest and education in Chicago's outstanding architecture. Its programs serve more than 350,000 people each year. For more information contact us at the address below, or visit us on our website:

Chicago Architecture Foundation

224 South Michigan Avenue

Chicago IL 60604

312-922-TOUR (8687)

www.architecture.org

ACKNOWLEDGMENTS

The Chicago Architecture Foundation is pleased to present *The Reliance Building,* primarily because it documents a building of the highest architectural importance, but also because it reflects a stunning recent restoration. Many people were involved in assembling this book.

Our gratitude goes to Hedrich Blessing, specifically Mike Houlahan and Bob Shimer, for their photographs. Thanks also to T. Gunny Harboe, AIA, Vice President of McClier's Preservation Group, for his assistance in chronicling the Reliance Building and its restoration, and to his colleague Doug Gilbert. We are also grateful to John Vinci and Ward Miller of Vinci/Hamp Architects, Inc., who were of great assistance in accessing the Richard Nickel Archive.

Thanks also to publisher Katie Burke and managing editor Eva Strock at Pomegranate Communications, whose faith in the CAF has made the Building Books series a reality.

For CAF's part, we would also like to acknowledge the work of in-house staff and freelancers, including Bonita Mall, vice president of programs; Ellen Christensen, architectural consultant; Jay Pridmore, author; and Ed Hirschland, editor, who also generously gave us access to his library.

Lynn J. Osmond, President and CEO

1890–1891 William Hale commissions Burnham & Root to design and begin construction on the fifteen-story Reliance Building on the southwest corner of State and Washington Streets. Because of leasing agreements, the building cannot be finished. In a feat of engineering, the base of the new skyscraper is completed beneath the upper three stories of the older First National Bank Building on the same site.

1891 Having worked on a design for the Reliance Building, John Root plans the World's Columbian Exposition, for which Burnham & Root had been hired to direct the design. Root dies unexpectedly of pneumonia at the age of 41, and Burnham quickly recruits Charles B. Atwood, of Boston, to take over as lead designer of the firm.

1895 The Reliance Building is completed as a steel-frame skyscraper. Its large windows and glazed terra-cotta cladding represent advanced architectural features. Its design, credited to Atwood, blends elements of the early Chicago skyscraper with Gothic-inspired ornamentation. Root's earlier design for the Reliance Building is unknown and has never been found.

1941 The Reliance Building has fallen into disrepair, but despite its condition, Swiss scholar Sigfried Giedion, a leading architectural historian of the era, calls it a milestone building despite its being "unnoticed in the history of architecture."

1994 With funding from the City of Chicago, exterior restoration of the Reliance Building is begun. Baldwin Development Company manages the project. Design and construction are carried out by a joint venture between McClier and UBM Inc.

1999 Canal Street Partners, LLC, acquires the Reliance Building from the city. The interior is restored under the architectural guidance of Antunovich Associates, with McClier as restoration architects. The building is converted into a first-class hostelry, Hotel Burnham, which becomes a landmark and commercial anchor of the burgeoning North Loop cultural district.

Among Chicago's monuments of architecture, none has a history quite so rich as the Reliance Building. When it was completed in 1895 it was, with fifteen stories, one of Chicago's tallest buildings, on one of the Loop's busiest sites. Its owner was a self-made man and developer known for standing up to corrupt aldermen, and its design was completed by two architects of nearly equal stature but almost totally opposite dispositions.

Since then the Reliance Building has been praised as a classic example of the Chicago School, buildings that expressed and did not hide their structure. The Reliance has been called the period's most direct precursor of modern architecture. Despite all that, it has also been neglected, left nearly derelict, threatened with demolition, and only later saved, restored, and converted into a luxury hotel.

The Reliance Building speaks volumes about both the history of architecture and the history of Chicago's character. When it was being built, the Reliance was a prime indicator of a building boom that overcame any and all obstacles to growth. When construction was complete, the Reliance dazzled Chicago with a gleaming enamel-white finish. It was a single shiny tower in a city of red brick buildings—distinctly modern not only in form but in function, with full electric service and a telephone in each office.

By the Great Depression, the Reliance had lost some glamour, and after World War II it fell into deep disrepair. But the building endured, perhaps owing to faint whispers of its glorious past. In 1941, for example, the

Photograph by Craig Dugan of Hedrich Blessing, courtesy McClier

The Reliance Building, completed in 1895 by architect Charles B. Atwood of D. H. Burnham and Co., is one of the most important early skyscrapers still standing. Its steel frame allowed for unusually large windows that let in lots of light. Once endangered, the Reliance Building is now an official Chicago landmark.

Imitation is said to be the sincerest form of flattery. One block north on State Street is an almost exact copy of the Reliance Building. The new building (bright white, with a row of five round windows under the cornice) was completed in 2000 and houses the Goodman Theatre, a restaurant, and a residence hall for the School of the Art Institute of Chicago. The architect is Laurence Booth of Booth Hansen Associates.

Photograph © Hedrich Blessing

Along Washington Street (looking west) the Reliance Building is nearly three-quarters of a century older than its Miesian neighbors like the Daley Center (right), but its steel frame and glassy curtain wall appear no less advanced in terms of modern architecture.

Postwar distress included marginal tenants above Karoll's Red Hanger Shop, a well-known clothing store in the 1960s and 1970s. For reasons of safety, the horizontal protrusion at the top, called the cornice, had been removed.

Age and neglect threaten buildings in many ways. Most serious in this case was the deterioration of the terra-cotta, cracked and blackening.

From eye level on the street, the Reliance Building was ignored, and it was relegated to mid- and low-level retail. But those who bothered to look up saw a work of architecture that even neglect could not deny.

distinguished Swiss scholar Sigfried Giedion explained in his landmark book *Space, Time, and Architecture* that the Reliance was "unnoticed in the history of architecture" but that it clearly foreshadowed the transcendent glass towers of the modern architect Ludwig Mies van der Rohe.

As time passed the Reliance was recognized as "a triumph of the structuralist and functionalist approach of the Chicago school," wrote the distinguished historian Carl Condit in 1964. Such praise was made poignant by the fact that the building was covered at the time with garish signs and occupied by tenants of questionable value, such as fortune-tellers.

By the 1970s, many historic structures had fallen, and the Reliance Building was creeping onto preservationists' "most threatened" lists. But it survived as if charmed. Plans were made to save and restore the Reliance to its glory as an outstanding example of the first generation of skyscrapers. Today the Reliance dominates a section of the North Loop, newly enlivened by theaters, restoration, and a collaboration between culture and commerce. Major funding was provided by the City of Chicago. It is a fitting monument for the district. The Reliance Building epitomizes "the challenge of the skyscraper," says Tim Samuelson, a leading authority on Chicago's historic structures. It is "functional, expresses its technology, expresses its time, its context, its use, and at the same time is a thing of beauty."

Now the Reliance Building is an optimistic symbol of a new spirit in Chicago's Loop, but more than that, it is a looking glass into our past that instructs, delights, cautions, and most of all renders a sense of permanence

Washington Street circa 1926 showed that the Reliance Building was
several steps ahead architecturally. But touches of the traditional made it
a comfortable neighbor and gentle harbinger of the future.

Photograph Richard Nickel, courtesy The Richard
Nickel Committee, Chicago

In the 1960s, the Reliance was nearly derelict when the preservationist-photographer
Richard Nickel photographed it inside and out, focusing on the Gothic quatrefoil design
that decorated the spandrels (facing page) and the wrought iron rails (above). Nickel
was a specialist in documenting great buildings before they were destroyed—he died in
1972 when Adler and Sullivan's Chicago Stock Exchange collapsed on him as he
attempted to get a few more photographs before its demolition. His death galvanized
the preservation movement and contributed to the saving of the Reliance Building.

In its decrepitude, the Reliance Building's tenant list deteriorated from bad to worse and then to almost none. The once stately office tower reached its low point in the 1980s, as shown on the facing page.

With restoration of the exterior, funded by the city and executed by McClier, terra-cotta was repaired, the surface was cleaned, and the roofline cornice was rebuilt. The result is a gleaming vintage skyscraper.

against which any fashion of the moment can be measured.

The Creative Developer

The Reliance Building was unique from the moment construction began, although at first less for its architecture than for the curious way in which it proceeded. Clearly, developer William Ellery Hale had the ingredients for a successful new building—a good site and good prospects for a major tenant on the ground floor. His problem was that he had an old four-story building on the site, easy enough to raze but with leases that were inconvenient or even impossible to break.

Obstacles be damned, Hale pushed forward with what today seems like a preposterous solution. He lifted the second, third, and fourth stories of the existing brick building on jackscrews and demolished the rest of the building at street level. He began the foundation and first floor forthwith, and in less than a year, a hybrid building was complete. He welcomed a new tenant, the dry goods store of Carson, Pirie, Scott & Co., into his modern new storefronts and left his old tenants on the jacked-up floors.

Impatience seldom leads to monuments, but Chicago in the 1880s and 1890s appears to have been an exception to the rule. Indeed, Chicago's Golden Age of architecture, as the period is often called, owed much to the need to build as quickly and profitably as possible. In 1871, the Great Chicago Fire destroyed

William Ellery Hale was an elevator mogul who became a Chicago developer and early proponent of the skyscraper.

the city's buildings but did not alter its soaring ambition. It triggered a surge of commerce and construction that challenged developers to keep up. They had to build quickly, and within the limits of the Loop—tucked between two branches of the Chicago River and Lake Michigan—they had to build tall.

Developers and their architects responded with various approaches. Perhaps most radical was that of architect William Le Baron Jenney, a former engineer of iron bridges during the Civil War. Jenney built what might have been the first metal-frame office building, the Home Insurance Building at LaSalle and Adams Streets. The Home Insurance was no artistic marvel, but it rose eleven stories and went up more quickly and more economically than much smaller buildings of standard masonry construction. The building—called by some the original skyscraper— was a stunning development and the first in the tradition in which the Reliance became an unforgettable landmark.

Creating tall office buildings required more than impatience, of course; it required taste and intelligence as well, not only from the architects but also from the developers who paid them. Hale was such a developer, with a biography similar to that of many individuals who built Chicago. As a young man, he migrated from New England to Wisconsin with his family. He made his first fortune through the sale of unglamorous commodities, primarily paper sacks for flour.

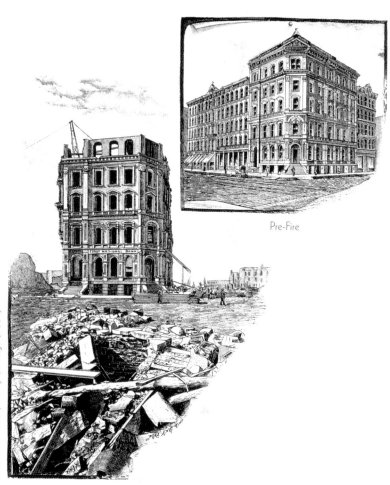

Pre-Fire

Post-Fire

From Royal L. La Touche, *Chicago and Its Resources Twenty Years After: 1871–1891* (1892)

The old First National Bank Building (facing page, pre-Fire drawing, top) was more than a mere predecessor on the Reliance Building's site. Left in ruins after the Chicago Fire of 1871 (post-Fire drawing), it was rebuilt and later purchased by developer George Ellery Hale in 1882. After planning the fifteen-story Reliance Building, Hale commenced construction by propping up the second, third, and fourth floors (where tenants had leases) on jackscrews and building the great glass storefront underneath. New tenant Carson, Pirie, Scott & Co., a dry goods store, occupied the lower storefront. The photograph above shows this hybrid arrangement, which persisted from 1891 to 1894.

Photograph by Jon Miller of Hedrich Blessing, courtesy
Antunovich Associates, McCaffery Interests, and McClier

When it was a first-class office tower, the Reliance Building's upper corridors featured mahogany trim and Carrara marble wainscoting. Floors were terrazzo. The Reliance Building reincarnated as Hotel Burnham includes new rugs and lighting fixtures of recent design (above and left) adapting the quatrefoil motif.

Before the Fire, Hale was drawn by Chicago's inexorable gravitational pull. Originally, his interest in buildings was tangential—Hale's second fortune was made in hydraulic elevators, a relatively new invention but a strict necessity for scores of new buildings that were soon to soar to the dizzying height of ten and more stories.

In the post-Fire construction boom, the Hale Elevator Company became an indispensable concern—and William Hale acquired sufficient wealth and stature to cut grafting politicians out of public contracts. Hale later left his elevator company to others and threw himself into real estate development, initially as a partner in large office blocks, including the Rookery on LaSalle Street, completed in 1888. As a result of his involvement in the Rookery as well as in other successful office building projects, Hale became well acquainted with the architecture firm that designed them, Burnham & Root. Hale concluded that it, with its principal designer John Wellborn Root, was the firm for him.

Hale understood that Root had lofty artistic aspirations; he was in search of a new type of American architecture and hoped to find it in the large office building. But he also knew that Root's aesthetics rarely if ever clashed with his clients' capitalistic intent. In his voluminous essays about urban structures, Root penned that the new architecture, ideally simple but expertly proportioned, would develop from the "rational and steady growth from practical conditions outward and upward toward a more or less spiritual expression." Hale rightly trusted Root's "rational" side and indulged the idea of "spiritual expression."

Collection of Edward C. Hirschland

The Reliance Building was State Street's most exciting landmark when it went up in 1895. The building was astonishingly modern, particularly in the context of its neighbors. The other buildings on the block, all of which were built after the Great Chicago Fire of 1871 and were less than twenty-five years old at the time, look old-fashioned in comparison

When Hale hired Burnham & Root to design the Reliance, together they envisioned something eminently functional. The ground floor would be spacious and feature large glass windows. Above would be additional retail space for smaller concerns, and higher still they imagined offices for doctors, dentists, and other professionals. Each tenant, they clearly decided, required a measure of luxury, but more important were practical comforts such as good elevators, modern electric service, and most of all—and this was emphasized by Hale—plenty of light. Hale's building was not planned as a palace. Rather, he wanted what the name "Reliance" implied: a building of substance, not grandeur.

The Practical Artist

Hale probably never suspected that the Reliance Building would enter the annals of architectural history. He did understand that whoever he hired to design it needed the skill to meet his definite requirements: to maximize floor space on a small lot, to capture enough sun to fill even lower floors with abundant natural light, and to build something of distinction if not beauty.

Many reasons made Burnham & Root the logical choice. One was that they already had some twenty Loop office buildings to their credit. Second, with Root's engineering intuition and architectural training, the firm had established itself as a master of steel-frame construction as well as the "floating" foundation—a reinforced concrete slab—that Root himself had invented. It minimized the unequal settling of large buildings in Chicago's terribly soggy soil.

Photograph by Craig Dugan of Hedrich Blessing, courtesy McClier

Among many marvelous tableaux of Chicago architecture, this one is taken from an entry in Marshall Field's State Street store and suggests that the Reliance Building, with its ribbons of glass, delicate ornament, and emphatic vertical thrust, is a true ancestor of America's newer and bigger skyscrapers.

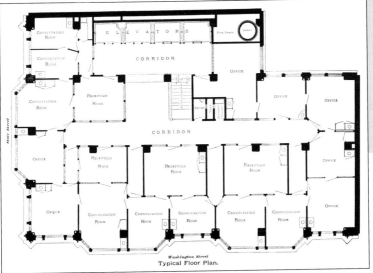

Typical Floor Plan.

Gossamer lightness was the hallmark of modern architecture as construction with steel frames and glass walls replaced the heavy stone and masonry of the nineteenth century. The structure is clearly seen in both the photograph on the facing page and the original floor plan above.

Root was also involved in establishing a style for Chicago skyscrapers, not a simple matter at the time. Indeed, the earliest tall buildings in Chicago showed little architectural luster. Many were like the Home Insurance Building, essentially a series of low-lying structures stacked one on top of the other—"like so many layers of cake," wrote critic William Jordy much later as he explained the development of true skyscraper architecture in Chicago. Root, on the contrary, was one of the first to recognize that new construction techniques must be tied to a new architectural look as well.

"Architecture is, like every other art, born of its age and environment," Root wrote in one of his many essays. "So the new type will be found by us, if we do find it, through the frankest possible acceptance of every requirement of modern life." Root was spiritual kin to Louis Sullivan, who was practicing at the same time and who wrote, "Form ever follows function." Root had his own way of putting it: "So vital has the underlying structure of these buildings become, that it must dictate absolutely the general departure of external forms."

Root's results represented an early development in the movement that became known as the Chicago School of Architecture. This term is used to describe a variety of commercial building styles featuring spare decoration and a careful sense of proportion. Root's skyscrapers became classics in this sense, perhaps culminating in the Monadnock Building, completed in 1892 after Root's death. The Monadnock (built with the old construction technique of masonry walls) seemed shocking at first because of its stark simplicity and absence of ornament. But its lines were so delicately wrought, and its function so uncompromising, that these features were quickly recognized as keynotes of the Chicago School.

Root's concept for the Reliance Building probably matched and may have outstripped the Monadnock in its blend of form and function. For the Reliance, Root chose steel framing—only recently perfected—for its security, ease of construction, and economy. Its narrow columns, moreover, created wide openings that met Hale's need for large windows and abundant light. Light and large display windows marked Root's design for the first-floor storefront and may have characterized his design for the upper stories as well.

A Classical Touch in a Modern Building

Sadly, John Wellborn Root died in 1891, some months before the base of the Reliance was completed. Burnham then recruited Charles B. Atwood, of Boston, to take over as lead designer of his firm. Atwood's selection was a switch for Daniel H. Burnham & Co. (as the firm was called after Root's death). Atwood was a classicist and reflected the taste that Burnham adopted as director of design for the World's Columbian Exposition. Chicago's great world's fair would be an elaborate fantasy of classical architecture, and Atwood eventually made what was arguably its most striking contribution, the Palace of Fine Arts, later rebuilt as the Museum of Science and Industry. While Atwood clearly enjoyed the re-creation of historical styles, the completion of the Reliance Building became his responsibility as well. And by 1895 he had put his

Daniel Burnham looks over the work of Charles B. Atwood. When John Root died in 1891, Atwood became lead designer of Burnham's firm and ushered in a revived interest in the classical and other styles modeled on the past.

Chicago Architecture Foundation Archive

The Reliance Building was one of the earliest skyscrapers framed
in steel, a recent advance over cast iron. Every effort was made to
create a frame of maximum rigidity—wind bracing was achieved
with 24-inch-wide girders riveted to the columns. Among
the advantages of steel construction was speed; the last eight
stories of the Reliance Building's frame went up in two weeks.

indelible mark on one of the most advanced commercial buildings of the nineteenth century.

Atwood's design for the Reliance Building, with its touches of French Gothic ornamentation, begs comparison to what Root would have done had he lived. Because Root's plans for the upper stories have been lost, we can only conjecture whether large expanses of glass within delicate frames would have continued from the street upward in the rest of his buildings. While Root is viewed as one of the most progressive architects of his time, history will never know whether his design would have presaged the age of glass and steel, later ushered in by Ludwig Mies van der Rohe, as Atwood's skyscraper certainly did.

What is known, however, constitutes rich architectural ironies. Indeed, it was Root who initiated the delicate Gothic-like motif in the ornamentation of the first floor, perhaps to provide the dry goods store that went in, Carson, Pirie, Scott & Co., with a touch of Old World elegance. Later it was Atwood, sometimes regarded as the antithesis of the original modern architecture, who oversaw the construction of a building that historian Carl Condit called "the structural culmination of the Chicago school."

Moreover, the most Atwoodian feature of the building, its white terra-cotta cladding, can be seen as the most advanced touch of all. Enameled terra-cotta was new in the early 1890s, and its promoters made strong claims for its function—that its smooth surface would wash itself "like a dinner plate" with each new rainstorm. For Atwood, its function was matched by the sculptural form and glimmering finish. Just two years after the dazzling White City of the

Close up and from certain angles, the Gothic character of the Reliance Building comes into view—here with delicate ornament amid clusters of narrow columns.

Photograph by Craig Dugan of Hedrich Blessing, courtesy McClier

The firm of Winslow Brothers became the leading supplier of ornamental metalwork in Chicago during the period of Chicago's vintage skyscrapers. The Gothic motif of the Reliance elevator grillage became a stock pattern in the Winslow catalog. Since Reliance developer Hale was also an elevator magnate, it can be assumed that the four elevators of his building were designed to set a standard that few other rental office blocks matched.

The elevator lobby of the restored Reliance Building was re-created by McClier, based largely on old photographs. Wrought iron, a mosaic tile floor, and six types of marble create a sense of openness in what is a relatively narrow space.

During the early skyscraper period, simplicity was key, but no detail was too small for the architect's attention.

Photograph © Hedrich Blessing

Wrought iron appeared traditional even in the nineteenth century, but its use was fashionable because of its handcrafted look and the way it allows precious light to pass through it.

Rich color and emphatic form were important to Chicago interiors when the Reliance Building was completed in 1895. Atwood Café in the new Hotel Burnham re-creates this taste for boldness and luxury.

world's fair, the architect completed this white skyscraper. Whatever else one concluded about the clash of progressive and historical styles, the Reliance stands as a harmonious blend of the functional Chicago School that followed the Great Fire and the elegant classicism that followed the great world's fair.

Restoring to Life

The successful restoration of the Reliance Building was completed in 1999 when the nineteenth-century skyscraper was converted into a first-class Loop hotel. As restoration stories go, this was a complex one, since a variety of obstacles presented themselves. Besides the building's advanced state of disrepair, which was becoming worse all the time, finding a suitable use for the building presented special problems. One obstacle was that the floors were small and unsuited for major commercial clients. Another was the wrought iron stairway running up the middle of the building; it was lovely and indispensable to the Reliance Building's historic architecture, but it was also difficult to secure and made conversion to rental offices problematic.

Yet another obstacle involved politics. As the city made an early commitment to save the building—this in the wake of the galling demolition of the historic McCarthy Building nearby—support from City Hall was not unanimous. Ambivalence about spending public funds on historic structures was expressed grotesquely when a Chicago alderman said that the city should take the $7 million being allocated to Reliance and blow up the building instead. "Then we can sell the land underneath and make some money on it."

The lobby of Hotel Burnham, designed by Antunovich Associates, makes use of wood finishes and ornamental metalwork. Its lavish sense of color is not too different from that of the Reliance Building's interior when it was new.

Photograph by Jon Miller of Hedrich Blessing, courtesy Antunovich Associates, McCaffery Interests, and McClier

Chicago's North Loop endured several decades of deterioration before it reemerged as a culture and arts district where the Reliance Building represents a major investment by the City of Chicago—and a major triumph.

The huge glass windows, which admit plenty of sunlight, were designed to remain shut. Bordering each of the large panes are two narrow vertical sashes that could be opened to allow cross-ventilation, a desirable feature in the days before air-conditioning. This tripartite arrangement is often called the Chicago window.

The white terra-cotta of the Reliance Building had the traditional touch of Gothic design, but its effect was also avant-garde as it reflected light in abstract ways, even as the building darkened and was forgotten by everyone but architectural enthusiasts.

The original masonry cornice of the Reliance Building was dismantled in the late 1940s because it was considered a hazard to pedestrians below. Its aluminum replacement was one of the final elements of the most recent exterior restoration. Insofar as the Reliance Building's profile was concerned, it was among the most important features.

The glazed terra-cotta cladding of the Reliance Building was one of its most modern features when built in 1895. Over time, it also proved to be the most fragile.

Photograph T. Gunny Harboe, courtesy McClier

Photograph T. Gunny Harboe, courtesy McClier

Compression forces conspired with moisture to crack tiles and corrode steel anchors. Of the twelve thousand pieces of terra-cotta that cover the building, two thousand were replaced, and another thousand were removed and reinstalled.

In the end, the Reliance Building prevailed. Its profound architectural character proved stronger than economic expediency. Indeed, the Reliance Building proved that almost nothing in preservation and restoration is expedient in the least. Painstaking work on the exterior was begun with funding from the City of Chicago as early as 1994 by McClier, overseen by the firm's preservation group's lead restoration architect, T. Gunny Harboe, AIA, and by the Baldwin Development Company. Together, by 1992 McClier and Baldwin had restored Burnham & Root's Rookery.

Work on the Reliance began as the transformation of the North Loop into an arts and culture district was realized. Happily, the city's approach to saving the building — restoring the exterior and then finding a buyer — worked. Canal Street Partners LLC (comprising McCaffery Interests, Mansur & Co., and Granite Developments) committed to the conversion of the building into what became Hotel Burnham, under the architectural guidance of Antunovich Associates. This project neatly matched tourism with Chicago's architectural history and led to what preservationists had been holding out for all along — a full-blown state-of-the-art restoration of the quintessential nineteenth-century Chicago skyscraper.

Yet, restoring the century-old monument required more than money. Also involved was uncompromising attention to the detail that originally had made the Reliance Building an icon. For the exterior, it meant finding and poring over old plans and photographs to authenticate details that would bring the building back to 1900, the year the restoration had targeted, when the Reliance Building was a fully functioning part of State Street.

Photograph by Jon Miller of Hedrich Blessing, courtesy Antunovich Associates, McCaffery Interests, and McClier

Modern elements of the Reliance Building include the transparency of its glass and the lively reflections thrown off by all its surfaces.

The pavement of marble mosaics in the elevator lobby was re-created in 1999, based on an original fragment that was found buried several inches below the existing floor.

Photograph © Hedrich Blessing

While building codes governing the 1999 restoration of the Reliance Building prohibited open-cage elevators, the metalwork is still a keynote of the interior of the present-day hotel. The upstairs grillwork (shown here) is original.

Stair rails and other ornamental ironwork in the Reliance Building were treated with the Bower-Barff process, in which metal is heated to 1600°F, and then superheated steam is passed over the surface. The result is corrosion resistance and an attractive bluish black appearance, as shown on the facing page.

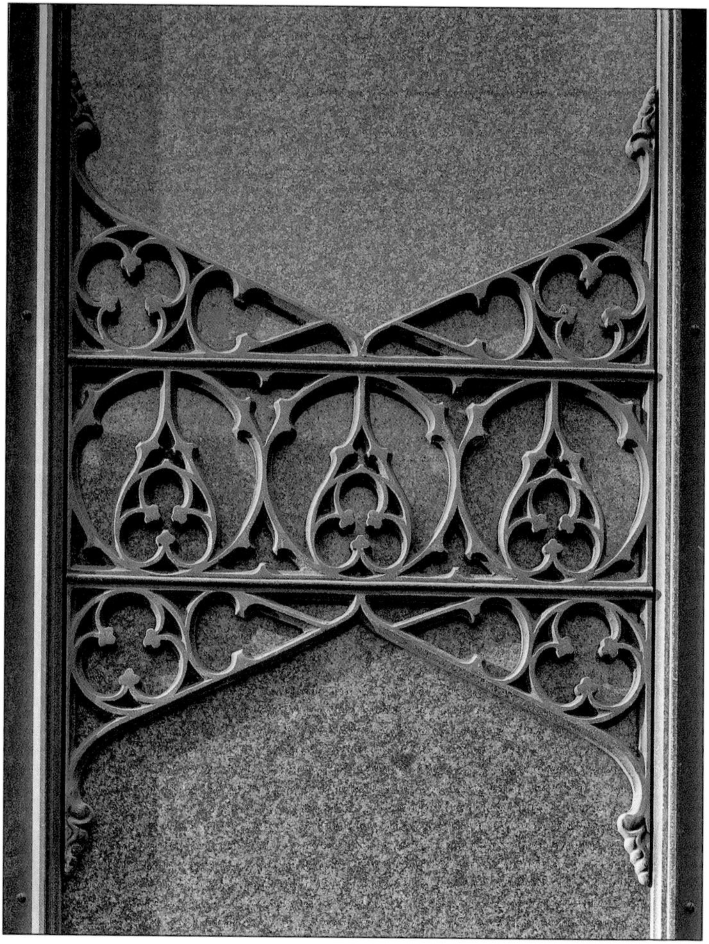

Photograph © Hedrich Blessing

Photograph by Craig Dugan of Hedrich Blessing, courtesy McClier

The red granite at the base of the building was quarried in Texas and is a close match with the Scottish original. The gothic quatrefoil design (detail, left) is a repeating motif that architect Charles Atwood used throughout the exterior and interior of the building. After the 1999 renovation, outdoor dining became a favorite feature of the Atwood Café.

Unknowns and educated guesses abounded as well. The red granite of the original base, believed to have been quarried in Scotland, was almost gone. Since virtually no granite is quarried anymore in Scotland, Harboe and his team found a replacement in Texas as close as possible in hue and tone. The new stone matches both a fragment of the original and, interestingly, the headstone on John Root's grave, hewn from the original quarry.

Inside, restoring and re-creating original details meant going through wrought iron catalogs, notably that of Winslow Brothers, who were leaders in the once-booming business of stair rails and elevator cages. Particularly puzzling were six different types of marble in vintage photographs of the building's lobby. Harboe compared one sample to marble used in other Chicago buildings of the era, and identified it as French *griotte* (burgundy marble with red and brown streaks). A fully restored interior was the result of dozens of such pieces of detective work.

The result is the return of the Reliance Building to what the developer and architects intended: a building with its aesthetic power restored and a new economic life of its own. The Reliance Building now stands as a model restoration, as close to the original as possible, but different in at least one significant way. This restoration shows that some effects of time cannot be erased. The passage of more than a hundred years has infused the Reliance Building, an elegant but simple Chicago skyscraper when it was built, with a distinct glamour in the twenty-first century that its original developer and architects probably never imagined.

Among six different types of marble in the elevator lobby, the dark burgundy in the lower wainscot is French *griotte*; the darkly veined panels shown here on the landing of the stair are of Italian *pavonazzo*.

The reception lobby of the Hotel Burnham reflects important keynotes of the Reliance Building: expanses of glass admitting abundant light as well as a measure of luxurious comfort in limited space.